CANADA
the people

Bobbie Kalman

A Bobbie Kalman Book
The Lands, Peoples, and Cultures Series

Crabtree Publishing Company
www.crabtreebooks.com

The Lands, Peoples, and Cultures Series

Created by Bobbie Kalman
For my mother, Valerie
You are the best!

Author: Bobbie Kalman

Editor: Adrianna Morganelli

Photo research: Crystal Sikkens

Editorial director: Kathy Middleton

Production coordinator: Margaret Amy Salter

Prepress technician: Margaret Amy Salter

First and second editions:

    Editors: Jane Lewis, Janine Schaub,
      David Schimpky, Lynda Hale
    Coordinating editor: Ellen Rodger
    Contributing editors: Carrie Gleason,
      Heather Macrae
    Production coordinator: Rose Gowsell

Cover: Many Canadians have friends from different backgrounds.

Title page: Canada is a multicultural country. Canadians come from many different cultural backgrounds.

Back cover: The beaver is one of Canada's national symbols.

Icon: A Haida killer whale carving.

Illustrations:

Scott Mooney: icons
David Wysotski, Allure Illustrations: back cover

Photographs:

First Light/Alamy: front cover
Anne Gordon Images: Anne Gordon: p. 5 (top left), 9 (top),
    21 (both), 23 (left), 27 (top); James A. Gordon: p. 20
Associated Press: p. 8
BigStockPhoto: p. 26, 31
Bryan and Cherry Alexander Photography: p. 4 (top)
Milt & Joan Mann/Cameramann Int'l., Ltd.: p. 19 (bottom)
Corbis/Magmaphoto: Annie Griffiths Belt: p. 22;
    Duomo: p. 25
Marc Crabtree: p.1, 15 (top left, bottom), 23 (right)
Betty Crowell: p. 14
Dreamstime: p. 7, 19 (top), 27 (bottom)
Glenbow Archives, Calgary (NA-670-45): p. 12
Beryl Goldberg: p. 15 (top right)
Industry, Science, and Technology Canada: p. 5 (top right),
    6, 29
Photo courtesy of David and Shilpa Jones: p. 17 (bottom)
Wolfgang Kaehler: p. 3, 9 (middle & bottom), 10, 28 (bottom),
    30 (bottom)
National Archives of Canada (C-057250): p. 13 (top)
Phil Norton: p. 30 (top)
Shutterstock: p. 4 (bottom), 5 (top right and bottom),
    13 (bottom), 16 (both), 18 (top), 28 (top)
Other images by Digital Stock

Every effort has been made to obtain the appropriate credit and full copyright clearance for all images in this book. Any oversights, despite Crabtree's greatest precautions, will be corrected in future editions.

Library and Archives Canada Cataloguing in Publication

Kalman, Bobbie, 1947-
    Canada : the people / Bobbie Kalman. -- Rev. ed.

ISBN 978-0-7787-9283-3 (bound).--ISBN 978-0-7787-9653-4 (pbk.)

    1. Canada--Social conditions--Juvenile literature.
I. Title. II. Series: Lands, peoples, and cultures series

HN103.5.K35 2010   j971   C2009-902567-1

Library of Congress Cataloging-in-Publication Data

Kalman, Bobbie.
  Canada. The people / Bobbie Kalman. -- Rev. ed.
    p. cm. -- (The lands, peoples, and cultures series)
  Includes index.
  ISBN 978-0-7787-9653-4 (pbk. : alk. paper) -- ISBN 978-0-7787-9283-3
(reinforced library binding : alk. paper)
  1. Canada--Social conditions--Juvenile literature. 2. Canada--Economic
conditions--Juvenile literature. I. Title. I. Series.

HN103.K35 2010
306.9073--dc22
                                2009017583

Crabtree Publishing Company

www.crabtreebooks.com   1-800-387-7650

Published in Canada
Crabtree Publishing
616 Welland Ave.
St. Catharines, ON
L2M 5V6

Published in the United States
Crabtree Publishing
PMB16A
350 Fifth Ave., Suite 3308
New York, NY 10118

Published in the United Kingdom
Crabtree Publishing
White Cross Mills
High Town, Lancaster
LA1 4XS

Published in Australia
Crabtree Publishing
386 Mt. Alexander Rd.
Ascot Vale (Melbourne)
VIC 3032

Contents

Faces of Canada

Imagine Canada as a huge patchwork quilt framed by the Atlantic Ocean on the east coast, the Pacific Ocean on the west, the Arctic Ocean to the north, and the United States to the south. The background of the quilt is a blend of mountains, plains, rivers, and lakes. The many faces of Canada's people are the exciting designs on each patch.

A mixture of people

Canada's population is a mixture of people from all kinds of cultural backgrounds. The first people to live on the land that is now called Canada were native peoples who came from Asia thousands of years ago. Europeans settled in Canada about five hundred years ago. Throughout Canada's more recent history, **immigrants** from Europe, Asia, and Africa have continued to come to Canada.

A multicultural nation

People from around the world have immigrated to Canada. The many different **cultures** represented in Canada add variety to the country's personality. This mixture of nationalities is called multiculturalism, which means "many cultures." Canadians try to celebrate and respect one another's culture.

(above) One-quarter of the world's Inuit population live in Canada's far north. Inuit also live in the Arctic regions of Russia, Greenland, and the United States.

(below) Many people in Canada look different from one another because they have different ethnic backgrounds. They have one thing in common—they are all Canadians!

Immigrant groups

The first immigrants to Canada came from France and Britain. Large numbers of Irish and Scottish people settled in the country soon after. Eventually, immigrants from dozens of different countries made their way to Canada. German, Italian, American, Greek, Portuguese, Ukrainian, Dutch, Polish, Asian, Indian, African and Scandinavian faces are just some of those that can be found in Canada today.

A safe refuge

Along with immigrant newcomers, Canada has welcomed refugees for many years. A refugee is a person escaping harsh conditions, war, or persecution in his or her own country. From African Americans fleeing slavery in the 1850s, to Kosovars leaving their war-torn country in the late twentieth century, Canada has often provided a safe place for thousands of people to call home.

(this page) Canada is known as an immigrant nation. It is home to native peoples as well as immigrants from many cultural and ethnic backgrounds

5

People have lived in the area that is now Canada for thousands of years. Some historians say the first Native peoples traveled to North America from Asia across a strip of land, called the Bering Strait, that once joined the two continents. Others argue that they came from South America and have lived on this continent for more than 40,000 years.

Many Nations

Thousands of years ago, the native peoples who lived in what is now called Canada were organized into twelve different groups, or nations. Within these nations were smaller groups, or bands. For example, the Iroquois nation, of central Canada, formed a confederacy, or large united group, made up of five different bands. Some nations formed alliances with other nations. Others fought with one another for land. Treaties were made between nations for trade, land, and peace agreements. A treaty is a formal agreement between two or more groups.

Community life

Native bands had their own forms of government and social organizations. Each person had a special role, but everyone worked together for the good of the community and the land. The lifestyles of the native peoples varied according to where they lived. Some bands were **nomadic**. Nomadic bands moved from place to place, following the herds of animals they hunted for food. Others lived in villages along the shores of Canada's many waterways. They used spears, nets, and hooks to catch fish to eat. Some groups settled in one place and grew vegetables, such as corn, beans, and squash.

The European influence

In the sixteenth century, Europeans were traveling to new lands to acquire wealth and claim land for their empires. When the British and French landed in North America, they changed the native way of life forever. Many native people died from diseases, such as smallpox, which were brought by the Europeans. Native people also died in wars fought between the British and the French. European settlers hunted and fished too much, causing the animals that native peoples needed for food, such as the buffalo, to become scarce. The effects of European settlement reduced the number of native people in Canada from 350,000 to about 100,000.

The lost people

In some cases, the arrival of the Europeans had a devastating impact on native peoples. The first native group to come into contact with Europeans was the Beothuk of Newfoundland. Diseases and cruel treatment by Europeans completely wiped out their people. The last Beothuk died of disease in 1829.

(left) The Inuit live in the Arctic.

(opposite page) A Native Canadian dressed in traditional clothing for a celebration.

Residential schools

One of the saddest parts of Native Canadian history was the forcible removal of thousands of native children from their families. Beginning in the 1800s, native children were taken from their homes and forced into residential schools. These schools were run by Christian churches and the Canadian government. At the schools, native children were taught about Christianity and made to follow the European way of life. Many children were treated badly at the residential schools. Today, these schools are no longer in operation. On June 11, 2008, Canada's **prime minister** Stephen Harper officially apologized to Native Canadians on behalf of the government for the residential school system. The Canadian government and native groups are still working to heal the damage that was done to native people in the residential schools.

Native Canadians today

There are 600 different bands of native people in Canada today. Most Native Canadians live on one of the country's many reservations. A reservation is a piece of land set aside for native people by the Canadian government. Some native communities have problems with poverty, and alcohol and drug abuse. Canada's native people are struggling to improve their living conditions and give their children a sense of pride in their culture. On June 29, 2007, they organized the first annual day of protest called the Aboriginal Day of Action. Events such as protests, rallies, and demonstrations were held throughout the country. The Aboriginal Day of Action calls attention to Native Canadian poverty, the poor quality of their social programs and healthcare, and land claim issues.

(above) Stephen Harper officially apologizes to the Native Canadians for the culture loss that resulted from the residential school system.

Self-government

In 1664, Native Canadians and Europeans signed a treaty called the Two-Row Wampum Treaty. The native peoples believed that this treaty gave Europeans the right to use some of their land, and that native people could continue living as they had before the Europeans came. Instead, the Europeans took control over native land and people. For many generations, Native Canadians have fought to regain control over their lands, laws, and culture. Native groups want each of their territories to be self-governed. Self-government would give native leaders control over education, healthcare, and social programs within their communities. In 1999, the first native self-governing territory, called Nunavut, was created in northern Canada.

(above) Native Canadians want their children to grow up with a sense of pride in their people and their land.

(below and left) The Haida on the west coast are known for their elaborate and colorful totem poles. Modern native artisans carry on the tradition of totem pole carving.

9

The first non-native people to reach the shores of Canada were the Norsemen. Leif Erikson, who came from either Iceland or Greenland, arrived around 992 A.D. and settled for a short time in what is now Newfoundland. Italian explorer Giovanni Caboto, or John Cabot, arrived on the same shores in 1497 and found the waters teeming with fish. Caboto sent word back to Europe and for a time, Portuguese, Spanish, and French boats came to the area to fish.

The French

The first Europeans to explore mainland Canada were the French. Jacques Cartier reached the Gulf of St. Lawrence in 1534. He may be responsible for naming Canada. The word "Kanata," an Iroquois word meaning village, appeared in Cartier's journals. Samuel de Champlain was the next to arrive. He founded Québec City in the early 1600s and Montréal in 1642. French settlers were encouraged to leave France and move to the Canadian colony. Some settlers became farmers, others were involved in the **fur trade**. The sale of furs and fish to France paid for the continued exploration and settlement of the area then known as New France.

The British

The earliest British immigrants to come to Canada were traders and explorers. In 1670, Britain sent a trading company, called the **Hudson's Bay Company**, into Canada. Britain and France fought for control over the land for many years. In 1713, a treaty granted control of French Acadia, which is now called Nova Scotia, and Newfoundland to the British. The wars continued, however, until 1763. At that time, another treaty gave all the French territory to Britain. New France became a British **colony** called Québec.

The United Empire Loyalists

The largest group of early British immigrants came to Canada during the American Revolution of 1775–1783. American colonists were fighting for independence from Britain. Some colonists, however, wished to remain loyal to Britain. About 50,000 of them, known as United Empire Loyalists, moved into Canada, which was a territory held by Britain. Soon after the Loyalists settled, many more immigrants from England, Scotland, and Ireland arrived.

Confederation

In 1867, the provinces of New Brunswick, Nova Scotia, Québec, and Ontario joined to form the Dominion of Canada under British rule. This was called confederation. Sir John A. Macdonald became the first prime minister of the new country. Over the next 40 years Manitoba, British Columbia, Prince Edward Island, Alberta, and Saskatchewan joined the confederation. Newfoundland, which joined in 1949, was the last province to become part of Canada.

(left) The town of Louisbourg in Cape Breton, Nova Scotia, was founded by the French in 1713. The Fortress of Louisbourg has been reconstructed and is now a National Historic Park.

African Canadians

Africans came to Canada as slaves of European travelers as early as 1608. Between 1776 and 1783, African American Loyalists came as both slaves and freemen from the United States and settled in Ontario and the Atlantic provinces. In 1834, a law made slavery illegal in Canada. Soon after, many slaves from America traveled hundreds of miles to Canada, seeking freedom.

The Underground Railroad

Many escaped slaves came to Canada by way of the Underground Railroad. The Underground Railroad was a network of people throughout the United States who did not believe in slavery. They helped African Americans escape to Canada. The Ontario cities of Windsor, Amherstburg, and Chatham were important railroad terminuses or end points. Harriet Tubman was the best known helper, or "conductor," along the Underground Railroad. Harriet Tubman lived in St. Catharines, Ontario, and helped more than three hundred American slaves escape.

Acadians

The first French settlement in Canada was called Acadia. During the wars between the British and French, the Acadians declared neutrality, meaning that they would not fight for either side. In 1775, Britain had control over Acadian land and demanded that Acadians take an oath to Britain. The Acadians refused. The British forced the Acadians to leave their farms, animals, and homes. This was called expulsion. Many Acadians were forced to move to the United States. The Cajuns who live in the American state of Louisiana are descendants of the Acadians.

(below) Thousands of slaves found freedom with the help of the Underground Railroad.

The West

The first Europeans to come to western Canada were fur traders. Large trading companies paid men for the furs of animals that they killed. During the nineteenth century, waves of immigrants from Europe and Asia cleared the land for farming.

European settlers

After Confederation in 1867, the Canadian government wanted to populate the country, especially the West. Immigrants from all over Europe were encouraged to come to Canada. In the 1890s, the government advertised inexpensive plots of farmland in the West to attract people from Russia, Romania, Belgium, Austria, Scandinavia, and the Ukraine. Often the settlers were given the land for free if they cleared the land and built a homestead. The government's immigration project was successful. Almost two million immigrants came to Canada between 1897 and 1911.

The Chinese and the railroad

Canada's first prime minister, Sir John A. Macdonald, helped unite the distant regions of Canada by building a railway across the country. In the 1880s, men came from China to help build the Canadian Pacific Railway.

Chinese laborers often worked on the most dangerous stretches of the railway. Some Chinese died in explosions while clearing the land for the tracks to be laid. Many of the Chinese workers sent for family and friends, and Chinese immigration increased. Eventually, **racism** and **discrimination** caused some Canadians to be afraid that there were too many Chinese coming to Canada. In 1923, the Canadian government passed the Chinese Immigration Act, which practically ended Chinese immigration for the next 25 years.

The Métis

During Canada's fur-trading days, some French and Scottish fur traders married Native Canadians. Their descendants, the Métis, are of mixed Native Canadian and European origins. Most Métis live in Manitoba and Alberta. Their religion is Catholic, but native customs and beliefs have been added. The language of the Métis combines Cree, French, and English words.

(below) Doukhobors are a religious group from Russia. Seventy-five thousand Doukhobors immigrated to the Canadian prairies in 1899. These Doukhobor women are plowing the land.

Japanese Canadians

Japanese people came to the west coast of Canada as early as 1877 to work as laborers, domestic servants, and fishermen. By 1942, there were 23,000 Japanese Canadians. During WWII, Japan and Canada were enemies. Despite the fact that many Japanese Canadians fought for Canada in WWI, there was a great deal of fear and mistrust of them during WWII. The Japanese Canadians living in British Columbia were sent to **internment camps**. Their businesses and properties were sold and families were separated. Men were sent to work on road crews and sugar beet plantations, while women and children were moved to deserted inland towns where living conditions were poor. In 1949, they were allowed to return to what was left of their homes.

Racism and apologies

In a country where people of many ethnic groups live together, racism can be a problem. Racism exists when a person of one race thinks that he or she is superior to a person of another race. Racial discrimination occurs when one person treats another differently or unfairly because of their race. Racial discrimination is against the law in Canada, but many people still feel that they are treated unfairly because of their race. Efforts are being made to make amends for unfair treatment of **minority** groups in the past. Recently, the Canadian government offered money to each survivor of the Japanese wartime internment. Today, Canada legally enforces multicultural rights to make sure that injustices like these do not happen again, and to make up for crimes committed in the past.

(top) During World War II, thousands of Japanese-Canadians were forced from their homes in British Columbia and into internment camps. These people are saying goodbye to friends and family before they are sent to camps.

(bottom) Canada is a multicultural country. Most of the time, Canadians respect one another's differences.

In the early 1900s, the Canadian government encouraged immigration mainly from European countries. More recently, Canada has welcomed people from Asia, the Caribbean, Latin America, South America, and Africa. Some newcomers are refugees, fleeing from hunger and war in their home countries. Other people come for the opportunity to live in a prosperous land.

Settling in

When new Canadians come into the country, many choose to live in the big cities. As job opportunities become available, some migrate to other areas of the country. Some immigrants settled in areas that resembled their homelands. For example, many Ukrainians were attracted to the **prairies**, while the Dutch tended to settle on the flat, fertile land of southwestern Ontario. Today, many Greek, Portuguese, and Asian immigrants settle in large cities such as Toronto and Vancouver. Large **ethnic** populations in the cities provide cultural support for newcomers. Certain neighborhoods of a large city have become characterized by stores and restaurants that focus on one ethnic group. Examples of these areas are Chinatown, Greektown, Little Italy, and Little India.

(below) In a small town in the Yukon called Watson Lake, visitors and residents have put up signs from countries all over the world. In the 1940s, a homesick American soldier put up one sign pointing in the direction of his distant hometown. Since then, thousands of signs have been added to the sign post at Watson Lake.

(above) African Canadians have been living in Canada since the seventeenth century.

(left) A Muslim girl in Vancouver. It is estimated that there will be more than one million Muslims living in Canada in 2010.

(below) Chinatown in Toronto reflects the large Asian population of the city.

Canadian families

Some people compare a family to the foundation of a building. If the foundation is strong, the building will be strong. In the same way, families are important in building a strong country. Canadian families have changed a lot in the past 50 years, but they are as important as ever.

Variety

The typical Canadian family is difficult to define. Some families are made up of two parents and any number of children. Others are made of single parents raising children on their own, either by choice or as a result of **divorce**. Blended families are those where one or both parents have children from previous relationships.

(right) Mixed families, in which parents are of different cultural backgrounds, are common in Canada.

(below) Often, members of the same family live on opposite sides of the country. Family reunions give family members the chance to keep in touch with one another.

Native families

Native societies are based on bands made up of large, **extended family** groups. Younger family members care for the older generation. **Elders** are the senior members of the family and community. They are respected for their knowledge and understanding of traditional ways and teachings. Elders pass on ancient knowledge, skills, and values to the young.

Marriage

Wedding ceremonies vary widely in Canada. Costumes, vows, food, and celebrations are all different depending on cultural **traditions**. A **Jewish** ceremony is completely different than a **Hindu** ceremony, which is different again from a Native Canadian ceremony. Many couples have weddings in traditional North American style, where the bride wears a white dress and has a number of bridesmaids. This type of wedding is often performed by a minister or priest in a church. Other couples have less formal ceremonies, held in someone's home or backyard. Some couples have no ceremony at all, and simply get married at their local city hall. Most Canadian weddings do have one thing in common—the event is a chance for family and friends to celebrate the union of two people.

Family reunions

Many families have large get-togethers called reunions. Family members, including aunts, uncles, and cousins, are invited. Sometimes relatives come from all over the globe to reunite with their family. One example of a big family reunion is the International Gathering of the Clans. This event is held once every four years in Nova Scotia. Participants from all over the world gather to share in traditional Scottish activities.

(below) This marriage is an example of Canada's multicultural population. The bride is of East Indian descent and a follower of the Jain religion, and the groom is of European and Native Canadian descent, and a Christian.

City life

Around 85 percent of Canada's population live in or near big cities. About one-third of Canada's total population live in its three largest cities: Toronto, Montréal, and Vancouver. City life can be fast-paced and hectic because cities are the centers of the country's business community.

City dwellers

Although there are large homes in big cities, many people live in small houses, apartments, or townhouses. People who live in big cities usually have less living space than those who live in **rural** areas. Neighbors may be close and many people often live in one dwelling. Tall apartment buildings are home to hundreds of families. Local parks often serve as the backyard. Public transportation, such as buses, streetcars, and subways, shuttle people around every day in large Canadian cities. Some cities are developing forms of "rapid transit" to get people from one place to another even faster.

(above) Residents of downtown Toronto are accustomed to traffic, noise, lights, and crowds.

(below) Most large Canadian cities have "green spaces," such as parks, which provide natural areas for city dwellers to enjoy.

Life in the suburbs

People who enjoy the benefits of living in a city but want extra space may choose to live in the suburbs. Suburbs are communities that surround the downtown core of a city. They consist of single-family homes, townhouses, and apartment buildings that are less crowded than those found in the city. Many of the people who live in the suburbs travel to the city center to work or attend school. This is called commuting. In larger cities across Canada, suburbs are as far as 30 miles (50 kilometers) from the city's core. Commuter trains and buses take people in and out of the city center.

Cottages and cabins

Some Canadian city-dwellers take advantage of Canada's beautiful scenery by owning or renting a cottage or cabin outside of the city. Cottages are sometimes thought of as "getaways" from the bustle of city life. Cottages are often located near rivers and lakes in less populated areas. They can be simple cabins for summer use, or larger homes that are also used in the winter.

(right) These colorful homes in downtown Montréal are built close together and have little yard space. Residents of Canadian cities who want large backyards often live away from the downtown area—in the suburbs.

(above) This cottage is located on a lake in British Columbia. During the summer, the family who owns this cottage escape their busy working lives in the city to go fishing, boating, swimming, and relax at the cottage.

Only a small percentage of Canadians live in rural areas. Some people who do not rely on a city for employment choose to live in the country. They prefer the quiet, wide-open spaces of rural Canada. Many of the people who live outside of cities are farmers. Life on a farm can be difficult and exhausting, but some still choose it over hectic city life.

A day on the farm

The Dalton family lives on a Holstein farm in Ontario. They have 50 head of cattle, and 25 laying hens. Hay, corn, and soybeans grow in the family's fields. In the summertime, when the Dalton children are on vacation from school, the whole family helps run the farm. The day begins at five a.m. when thirteen-year-old Amanda and her father collect the cows from the field and lead them into the milking parlor in the barn. They direct the cows into metal stalls, called stanchions. Once in the stalls, the cow's udders are washed with disinfectant and slipped into the sockets of the automatic milking machine. Milking takes about an hour and the cows are fed from a trough while they are being milked. The automatic milking machines make it easy for just two people to milk 50 cows at once.

While the milking is going on, Amanda cleans up the milking parlor and bottle feeds the newborn calves. Amanda waters the cows, which means she gives them a drink, and feeds them hay and **silage**.

(below) When the Dalton's Holstein cows are not in the barn being milked, they roam (or rest) in the field next to the farm.

Amanda's older brother Jason drives the tractor to collect the hay and silage for the cows. Jason and his father do most of the work on the small fields that the family owns. The crops are grown mostly to provide food for the cows, but some of the soybean crop is sold for extra money.

Amanda's mother and younger brothers wake up early as well. They feed the chickens and collect their eggs—some to eat, and some to sell at the farmer's market. They make breakfast for the older children and Mr. Dalton.

Afternoons on the farm are spent with the whole family in the fields planting, fertilizing, or harvesting—depending on the time of year. After another meal for the family, the milking and watering chores are all repeated.

A difficult challenge

Farm life involves long days of hard physical labor. The entire family is involved in order to keep the farm running smoothly. It is very difficult for small family farms to compete with big, commercial farms that produce larger crops using expensive equipment. Commercial farms can produce more, which means that they can afford to sell crops for less money. Since the 1990s, it has become more difficult for Canadian family farms to survive. Many people in Western Canada had to sell farms that had been in their family for generations. Western farmers asked the Canadian government to help them continue farming.

(above) When Amanda is not doing chores, she looks after Banjo, the family's puppy.

(left) Amanda's uncle Ron sometimes helps her father with farm work.

 # School

Canadian children begin their education at five years old. Their first year of school is called kindergarten. At most schools, children can start a year earlier with a program called junior kindergarten. After kindergarten, students attend eight grades of elementary school. They study traditional subjects such as math, science, reading, and social studies. They also learn about computers, perform plays, take field trips to museums and historic sites, and play sports.

High school

After the eighth grade, students go on to high school, where they can choose many of the subjects they want to study. They take classes that will prepare them for university, community college, or a job. School clubs, concerts, team sports, and dances make secondary school more fun. Some schools offer students classes in music, ballet, or theater. Of course, the students still have to study regular academic subjects.

Different kinds of schools

There are many kinds of schools in Canada. Public schools are funded by **taxes** paid by Canadian citizens. Most Canadian children attend public schools. Private schools are often run by religious groups, who wish their children to receive religious teachings. Some of these schools, such as the Roman Catholic schools in Ontario, are funded by tax dollars, while others are privately funded by members of the religious community. There are also private schools in Canada that use alternative teaching methods. An example of this type of private school is the Montessori school. Montessori schools have small classes, and children of different ages study in the same room. Students are encouraged to learn independently and develop at their own rate.

(above) Some Canadian schools require that students wear uniforms. At this school in British Columbia, students wear uniforms every day.

Education for native peoples

Native children who live in isolated communities go to schools that are operated by the **federal government**. Native children who live in more populated areas are educated within their own communities. In addition to regular classes, they learn the language of their **ancestors** and traditional skills.

French language schools

In Québec, most students are taught in the French language. Students outside of Québec can attend French immersion schools. These schools offer classes that are taught completely in French, from kindergarten to high school. Some public schools offer French immersion programs within their regular English schools.

Universities and colleges

Canadians who wish to continue their education can choose from community colleges, universities, institutes of technology, or institutes of applied arts and sciences. Students in Québec attend colleges called CÉGEPs for two or three years before they go to university. Community colleges train students for specialized jobs, such as computer programming, fashion design, plumbing, or photography. Universities teach students how to gain knowledge in the arts and sciences. Teachers, doctors, lawyers, and dentists go to university to train for their professions. Forty percent of Canadian students who continue their education past high school attend university, while sixty percent go to college.

(left) The University of Guelph is one of 22 universities in Ontario.

(below) At this Muslim private school, children also learn about religion.

Haley's skating lesson

Haley has just hit the snooze button on her alarm clock for the second time when she hears her stepfather calling from the kitchen, "Wake up lazy bones, it's 8:15!" Haley is thinking about how she hates waking up in the morning, but then she remembers that today is her first figure skating lesson! She leaps out of bed, gobbles up her cereal and juice, brushes her hair, and grabs her backpack.

Haley is a grade seven student in Winnipeg, Manitoba. Her mother, a high school science teacher, has already left for work. Haley's half-brother Finlay is in grade two. They attend the same public school, which is about a mile from their house. Haley's stepfather, Chris, is studying at university to become an accountant. He will drop the children off at school before he leaves for his classes.

When Haley arrives at school at 9:00 a.m., she tells her best friend Rowan how excited she is about her first skating lesson. Haley says, "I'm going to be a famous figure skater some day!" Rowan laughs and tells Haley that she has chosen swimming as her after school activity. Both beginner programs are offered through their public school. Haley has been delivering newspapers for six months to help pay for the lessons and her skates.

Haley can hardly wait for her lesson, but has a full day of classes to attend first. During her least favorite subjects, geography and science, she can hardly sit still. During math class, which she likes, she manages to focus on solving the problems her teacher gives the class. Music and French are fun, but when the bell rings at 3:30 p.m. she is the first student out the door.

(below) Haley and her friend Amanda take skating lessons after school.

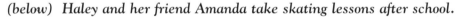

Haley's lessons are being held at the skating rink across the street from her school. She arrives at the rink and changes into her skates and warm-up suit. She meets her new coach and the six other girls in her class. The coach instructs the girls to begin running laps around the rink to warm up. After the warm-up, the girls spend about half an hour talking to the coach about what they will be learning. Her coach says that they will begin by learning about forward stroking, backward stroking, and skating on one foot. Haley wants to start skating right away but knows that she has to be patient. The coach leads Haley through some stroking exercises and her first lesson is already over. Haley races home to find her mother getting spaghetti ready for dinner. "How was your very first skating lesson?" her mother asks. Haley tells them that it was great. After dinner, Haley does her homework and then watches some television until it is time for bed. At 10:00, Haley drifts off to sleep dreaming about a cheering crowd throwing flowers onto the ice after she finishes a brilliant figure skating performance.

(below) **Haley dreams of skating in the Olympics one day.**

Canadian cuisine

The story of Canadian food begins with the native peoples. Largely hunters and gatherers, the Native Canadians survived on game meats such as caribou, deer, and bison. Some groups cultivated corn, squash, wild rice, and beans. Dried fruit and nuts were also part of the native diet. Native Canadians shared their recipe for pemmican with early French explorers. Pemmican is a meal of dried meat, fat, dried fruit, nuts, and honey. It gave the explorers the extra energy they needed to sustain them on long canoe voyages.

Flavors of many countries

Today, the multicultural flavor of Canada is reflected in Canadian cuisine. Canada is lucky to have groups of immigrants who have preserved delicious recipes as part of their cultural **heritage**. The English still savor their steak and kidney pie, the Italians their pasta, and the Polish their *pierogi* and sauerkraut. People from the Caribbean make roti, which is spiced meat wrapped in flat bread. Asian cooks have made tofu, noodles, curry, and sushi common menu items. Some Native Canadians still include game meat in their meals. Bannock, a kind of flat bread, and wild rice dishes are also staples of the Native Canadian diet.

Canadiana

Along with the specialties of other countries, there are some Canadian standards. Fast foods such as hot dogs, hamburgers, and french fries are available all over the country. Meat and potatoes, pie, and ice-cream are commonly found on Canadian dinner tables. Fish is popular, and it is available in abundance. British Columbia salmon is well known and liked, although overfishing has made it more difficult to find. *Tortiere*, a meat pie, is a traditional French Canadian food. Poutine, or french fries served with cheese curds and gravy, is a French Canadian favorite.

Maple syrup festivals

Maple syrup is probably one of the best known Canadian food items. The delicious syrup is made from the sap of maple trees that grow mainly in Québec and Ontario. At sapping time, usually in late winter, maple syrup festivals are held to celebrate the sweet harvest. Maple syrup festivals in Ontario and Québec feature craft vendors, food, and plenty of pancakes with maple syrup. The festivals usually attract thousands of visitors.

Blueberry pancakes

Here's a chance to try that delicious Canadian maple syrup on some blueberry pancakes! Ask an adult for help.

2 cups (475 mL) blueberries
2 1/4 cups (535 mL) all-purpose flour
3 teaspoons (15 mL) baking powder
1 teaspoon (5 mL) salt
4 tablespoons (60 mL) sugar
2 eggs, well beaten
1 1/2 cups (355 mL) milk
6 tablespoons (90 mL) melted butter

Combine flour, baking powder, salt, and sugar in one bowl. Combine the egg, melted butter, and the milk in a second bowl. Make a hole in the center of the dry ingredients and pour in the wet ingredients. Blend gently with a fork. Try to use as few strokes as possible to mix the ingredients. Don't worry about the lumps. Too much mixing will make the pancake batter rubbery! Brush the frying pan lightly with vegetable oil or melted butter. Heat the pan so that water droplets dance when dropped into the middle. Pour 1/4 cup (60 mL) of batter into the pan and wait for bubbles to appear. When the bubbles start to burst, drop a small number of blueberries onto the pancake. Then flip over the pancake. Cook for another minute or so. You can put your finished pancake on a plate in the oven, on low heat. That way your pancakes will stay warm while you cook the rest. *Bon appetit!*

(opposite page) A Canadian family eats a turkey dinner with corn on the cob.

(above) This woman is gathering sap from maple trees. The sap will be used to make maple syrup.

(below) Follow the recipe, and make your own great blueberry pancakes!

Watching television, reading, making crafts, listening to music, attending cultural events, playing sports, and visiting friends are some ways in which Canadians spend their leisure time. The cold winters, warm summers, and beautiful landscapes of Canada make it possible for people to enjoy indoor and outdoor activities.

Popular winter sports

Exciting winter sports make the long, cold Canadian winter a season of fun! Skiing is a sport that is well suited to Canada's mountains and forests. Downhill skiers and snowboarders take a lift to the top of a mountain and then swoosh down at great speeds. Cross-country skiers prefer to travel at a slower pace on a forest trail. Some Canadians enjoy the thrill of snowmobiling. Skating and hockey are also favorite Canadian winter sports. Skating rinks can be found in every town and city.

(left) Ice skating is fun on frozen ponds and lakes, artifical rinks, and indoor arenas. The pond at Nathan Phillips Square in Toronto serves as a skating rink in the winter.

(below) Downhill skiing is enjoyed on Canada's many mountains and large hills.

Hockey

Ice hockey is a popular Canadian sport that inspires passion in players and spectators. Canada has six hockey teams in the National Hockey League, including the Montréal Canadiens and the Toronto Maple Leafs. The most famous Canadian hockey player of all time is Wayne Gretzky. Known as "The Great One," Gretzky broke scoring records and drew crowds through the 1980s and 1990s. He played for the Edmonton Oilers until 1988 when he was transferred to the Los Angeles Kings. Gretzky played for the New York Rangers until he retired in 1999.

Lacrosse

Canada's official national sport is lacrosse. Originally played by the native peoples, lacrosse is a running sport in which two teams attempt to score by throwing a small ball into each other's net. Players use long sticks that have woven leather baskets on the end to carry, catch, and throw the ball.

Spectator sports

Canadians enjoy watching professional sports. Baseball, basketball, and hockey are three favorites. World Series champions in 1992 and 1993, the Toronto Blue Jays baseball team attracts large crowds at the Rogers Centre in Toronto. The game of basketball is also popular, and was even invented by a Canadian! James Naismith, born in Ontario, invented basketball in 1891. While working as a teacher in Springfield, Massachusetts, Naismith created the game as a way to keep a group of students busy. Canada joined the National Basketball Association or NBA in 1995. The Toronto Raptors' team colors are bright red, purple, black, and "Naismith" silver, in honor of the sport's inventor.

On the move

Canadians love to travel! University students often backpack around the world before they begin their careers. Some young people fly to Europe, Asia, Australia, or South America to explore historic sites and experience different ways of life. Others take road trips around Canada and the United States. Florida, Mexico, and the Caribbean islands are favorite destinations of families looking for a warm vacation to escape the cold winter. In the summers, many Canadians prefer the peace and beauty of the Canadian wilderness. They enjoy camping trips in Canada's many parks.

(this page) Kayaks and canoes were invented by the native peoples. Kayaking is still a popular way to explore the wilderness areas of Canada.

Canada is a country blessed with abundant natural resources, a strong workforce, and a stable economy. Canada's future depends on overcoming several challenges. These problems are not new; their roots go far back in history.

The treatment of native peoples

Native Canadians have experienced much injustice at the hands of non-Native Canadians. Today, the native peoples who live on reserves are assisted by the federal government. Even with the help of the government, however, life is difficult. Until recently, many Native homes lacked running water and flush toilets. Sometimes as many as twenty people would live in a two-room house. Problems such as unemployment, family violence, poor health conditions, drug abuse, and suicide are being addressed by native leaders.

(above) This Inuit girl lives in northern Canada. Native groups in Canada are working to reclaim control over their lands and people.

Improving the situation

Native groups, together with the federal government, are working to improve life for native peoples. Many reservations are now governed by traditional leaders, such as a chief or a council of elders. Some reservations have native police and counseling services. Several now offer health care treatment based on traditional healing methods. Despite these efforts, there is still much to be accomplished.

French and English relations

Another challenge facing the future of Canada is that of French-English relations. Some French-speaking people in Québec want to separate from Canada and form their own country. Other Canadians, however, believe that Québec is an important part of Canada and do not wish to see the country split apart.

Environmental issues

Canadians use more energy per person than any other people in the world. Canadians also produce a lot of garbage. This garbage is piling up at waste-disposal sites called landfills. Some landfill sites are almost full, and cities are running out of places to dump their garbage. **Emissions** from vehicles and factories contribute to air pollution. Big cities such as Toronto, Vancouver, and Montréal are often covered in smog. Old growth forests have been clearcut for lumber. Canadian waterways have been polluted by city, farm, and factory wastes.

Pollution solutions

Today, many Canadians are committed to taking care of the environment. Government and local programs have been set up to protect wildlife and forests, clean up industrial waste and pollution, and **conserve** vital sources of energy. Recycling and reforestation projects have support countrywide. National parks, which preserve and protect wildlife and natural areas, will one day cover close to three percent of the country.

Health care

When Canadians are sick or injured, most of their medical bills are paid by provincial health insurance, even if they are in the hospital for a long time. The health-care system guarantees that Canadians receive treatment according to their needs and not their ability to pay. In recent years, people have become concerned that the health care system is failing to meet the needs of Canadian citizens. Provincial governments are looking at ways to improve the system.

(above) This old-growth forest on Vancouver Island was destroyed by clearcutting.

(opposite page, top) This man is holding the Canadian flag and the Québec flag. One of Canada's most serious issues is separatism. There are many people in the province of Québec who feel that separating from the rest of the country will help preserve French culture. Other Canadians hope that French Canadian concerns can be solved, instead of splitting the country apart.

Glossary

ancestor A person from whom one is descended

Arctic The region surrounding the North Pole

colony A territory governed by a distant country

conserve To protect from loss, harm, or waste, especially of natural resources

culture The customs, beliefs, and arts of a distinct group of people

discrimination The act of treating a person or group unfairly based on a characteristic such as race or gender

divorce The legal ending of a marriage

elder A senior member of a native group

emissions Substances, such as engine exhaust, that are sent out into the air

ethnic Describing a group of people who share a common culture, race, or origin

extended family A family group that includes parents, children, uncles, aunts, cousins, and grandparents

federal government The central, or main, government of Canada

fur trading The business of acquiring animal furs, by trapping them or trading with native peoples. Fur traders would then sell the furs to large companies that would make and sell items such as beaver hats

heritage The customs, achievements, and history passed on from earlier generations

Hindu Followers of an ancient Indian religion based on the holy books called the *Vedas*

Hudson's Bay Company A fur-trading company that once controlled most of western Canada

immigrant A person who settles in a new country

internment camp A confined area where prisoners are kept during a war

Inuit Native people who live in Canada's Arctic

Jewish People who follow the religion of Judaism, which believes in one God

Métis A group of people who are of mixed native and European origin

minority A small group of people within a larger group

nomadic Describing a person or group that travels from place to place in search of food

prairies A region of Canada characterized by flat, treeless grassland

prime minister The head of Canadian government

racism A belief that one race is superior to another

rural Describing something in the country

silage Food for livestock

tax Money collected by the government that is based on property, income, services, or purchases

tradition A long-held custom or belief

Index

Printed in China — CT